Poems of a Soul

to the Sacred and Blessed Heart of Jesus

Poems of a Soul

to the Sacred and Blessed Heart of Jesus

DIVINE MESSENGERS
Collection

**Poems transmitted by the Glorified Christ Jesus
to the visionary Friar Elías del Sagrado Corazón de Jesús,
in July and August of 2018**

Mother María Shimani de Montserrat
Friar Elías del Sagrado Corazón de Jesús

Shasti Association

Copyright © 2020, 2021 Mother María Shimani de Montserrat
Original title in Spanish:
Poemas de un Alma al Sagrado y Bendito Corazón de Jesús
The profits generated from sales of books by Trigueirinho and his associates will be used to support the non-profit activities of the Shasti Association and to disseminate their work.

Cover, translation, editing and design:
Volunteers of Irdin Publishing Association
and Association Mary, Mother of the Divine Conception
Original cover painting by Gabriel Souza

Cataloging-in-Publication data

Mother María Shimani de Montserrat, Friar Elías Del Sagrado Corazón de Jesús
Poems of a Soul to the Sacred and Blessed Heart of Jesus
96 p.
ISBN: 978-1-948430-11-1
Library of Congress Control Number: 2021953311
1. Religion/Spirituality
2. Body, Mind, Spirit/Prophecy
3. Religion/Bible Studies

English language rights reserved

Shasti Association
P.O. Box 318
Mt. Shasta, CA 96067-0318
editorial@shasti.org
www.shasti.org

Shasti Association

Contents

About the visionaries 07
Introduction 09
The Request of Christ Jesus 10
Prologue 11

First Series of Poems

First Poem 14
Second Poem 16
Third Poem 18
Fourth Poem 20
Fifth Poem 22
Sixth Poem 24
Seventh Poem 26
Eighth Poem 28
Ninth Poem 30
Tenth Poem 32
Eleventh Poem 34
Twelfth Poem 36

Second Series of Poems

First Poem 40
Second Poem 42

Third Poem	44
Fourth Poem	46
Fifth Poem	48
Sixth Poem	50
Seventh Poem	52
Eighth Poem	54
Ninth Poem	56
Tenth Poem	58
Eleventh Poem	60
Twelfth Poem	62

Third Series of Poems

First Poem	66
Second Poem	68
Third Poem	70
Fourth Poem	72
Fifth Poem	74
Sixth Poem	76
Seventh Poem	78
Eighth Poem	80
Ninth Poem	82
Tenth Poem	84
Eleventh Poem	86
Twelfth Poem	88

About the visionaries

Mother María Shimani de Montserrat

Consecrated nun of the Grace Mercy Order and visionary dedicated to bearing witness to the instructions of the Divine Messengers (Christ Jesus, the Virgin Mary and Saint Joseph), a spiritual task that she develops in different places of the world, forming and guiding groups of prayer and altruistic service.

She is a member of the Council of Regency and Permanent Guidance of the Fraternity – International Humanitarian Federation (FIHF) and the Grace Mercy Order, institutions dedicated to prayer and to selfless service. She coordinates the activities of the Light-Communities and the Marian Centers in Argentina, Brazil, Portugal and Uruguay.

She gives lectures focused upon the current planetary situation and the multiple possibilities of humanity drawing closer to spiritual life through prayer and charity. She is the author of the books **Mensajes del Gran Reino Celeste, Siete días con el Maestro Jesús de Nazareth, Mensajes de Paz**, (**Messages of Peace**, also published in English) **Mensajes de Misericordia, Mensajes de Humildad,** and **Cristo de la Luz, Samana Redentor**, all published by Irdin Publishing.

Friar Elías del Sagrado Corazón de Jesús

Consecrated monk of the Grace Mercy Order and visionary, he dedicates his life to prayer and selfless service, following the indications of Christ Jesus and the Virgin Mary.

He was contacted by the Most Holy Virgin at the age of seven and since then he has been prepared by Her for the public task, which began in 2011.

He participates in meetings of prayer in different countries to propagate the words of the Divine Messengers. He is the author of the books **Mensajes de Paz** (**Messages of Peace**, also published in English) and **Mensajes de Misericordia**, both published by Irdin Publishing.

Introduction

During the months of July and August of 2018, Christ Jesus transmitted a set of poems called *Poems of a Soul to the Sacred and Blessed Heart of Jesus* through the visionary Friar Elías del Sagrado Corazón de Jesús, a monk of the Grace Mercy Order. In this book, three series are gathered, comprising thirty-six poems altogether.

It is important to highlight that in the initial period of the approach of the Divine Messengers to the visionary monastics of the Order, the Virgin Mary requested Mother María Shimani de Montserrat, as an instructor, to accompany the process of contact of Friar Elías, and to also be in charge of the organization of all the instruction that composes this work, "Divine Messengers Collection." For this reason, the two visionaries are listed as authors of this book.

Upon these pages are printed simple but profound words, which express devotion and faith. These poems will be of help for those who want to approach the Sacred Heart of Jesus and enter the mystery of His infinite Love.

May they be an instrument of meditation and prayer for those who aspire to follow the teachings of Jesus and return to the Heart of God.

The Request of Christ Jesus

"In the name of the Will of God, I come to ask
that all souls of the world, all those who request it
as well as those who do not request it, may receive the book
of My Poems of the devotion of a soul to the Sacred and Blessed
Heart of Jesus, because in the most definitive hours,
in which you will find yourselves before God and facing
unimaginable things that will be seen throughout the world,
you will withdraw into your rooms, light a candle
and, in the name of your Guardian Angels, you will pray these poems
so that the Divine Grace and the Mercy of the Father
may sustain this planet and mainly,
all of your inner worlds.

Because when I am no longer with you, as I am with you today,
your fortitude will not only be My Heart
but also all the words that I have said to you.

Within the Poems lies the key of your transformation.

I will be grateful if this is delivered as soon as possible
and propagated throughout the whole world, in all
possible languages, as a means of reparation of the hearts
of the world to the Sacred and Blessed Heart of Jesus."

*Passage from the Apparition of Christ Jesus
on August 16, 2019, in Buenos Aires, Argentina*

Prologue

*Transmitted by the Glorified Christ Jesus in the
Marian Center of Aurora, Uruguay, on August 21, 2018*

That someday, My followers, you may be fully encouraged to imitate this soul, not only in the sweetness of its words but also in the way of living them, one by one.

I would like you to be so similar to this soul, in devotion, purity and sincerity because, beyond the imperfections of life and of human appearances, in the depths of each being there is an inner Christ capable of conducting your lives and your souls towards My Celestial Church.

I hope to listen to poems so similar to these, yet at the same time simple and true, that may spring from your hearts so that one day I may be able to rescue that which your souls could give Me internally while praying and speaking to Me with the transparency of heart.

I encourage you to be part of this legacy of the redeemed who, having gone through great confirmations, unexpected challenges and extensive tests, confirmed themselves, day by day, to My Sacred Heart.

I need that, finally, the new Christic legacy of each heart in transformation may be available for its Master and Lord.

May each heart that is encouraged to talk to Me like this precious soul be able to express the love and inner reverence that it feels for Me. Thus, I will be able to gradually manifest on the surface of the Earth the new brotherhood of Christs.

I thank you for keeping My Words in your hearts!

Who blesses you,

Your Master, Christ Jesus

First Series of Poems

First Poem

First Series - July 8, 2018

Beloved and kind Heart of Jesus,
Lord of Mercy and Peace,
draw my heart towards Yours.

May I be one in You
to be one with my brothers and sisters.

Meek Heart of Jesus,
become part of me without conditions or forms.

Break down within me
the walls that separate me from the light of truth.
Heal my blindness that has led me to pride.
Cure my heart that has been led to constant suffering.

Most loving and pure Heart of Jesus,
may Your Flame of Love dissolve all doubts.

May the Flame of Love that springs
from the center of Your humble Heart
be the light that dissipates the darkness from my fragile heart.

O most loving Shepherd and Guide of hearts!
may the Rays that spring from the Wounds of Your Hands
illuminate the pathway that will lead me to redemption.

May I always be able to find refuge in Your Heart
and may I also find this refuge, with trust,
in my brothers and sisters,
because I only aspire and long for the good,
in me and in all beings.

Peaceful Heart of Jesus,
You, who gestate new things within human beings,
You, who renew and vivify everything that
You touch with Your holy Hands,
may the Ray of Your strict obedience
and of Your divine purity invade me.

Teach me, Jesus, to love as You love us and have loved us.

Help me, my Jesus, to be only an instrument in Your Hands
so that at least a small spark of my consciousness
may serve Your magnificent Work of Love and Forgiveness.

Teach me, my Jesus, to be just and to not be indifferent.

Teach me to imitate You and represent You,
just as You, humble Master,
have represented the Celestial Father on Earth.

Meek Heart of Jesus, appease me.
Sweet Heart of Jesus, tame me.
Eternal Heart of Jesus, console me
and give me the strength of Your Divine Spirit
in the hours of great tests,
because everything must return to You, Lord.
Everything belongs to You forever.

Amen.

Second Poem

First Series - July 9, 2018

Make me love the Divine Purpose, Lord,
as You have loved it since the beginning
while You were among us as a Child,
while You preached and taught the Word of Life,
while You worked and did wonders in the most closed hearts.

Beloved Jesus,
faithful Master and Celestial Spouse,
commit my life more and more to You.

During the cold night, may I feel the warmth of Your embrace,
may I always take refuge in Your Heart
when I cross the desert of the soul,
may I be absolutely empty
each time You call me to serve.

Venerable and noble Heart of Jesus,
participate entirely in my life,
because my life is Your life,
my breath is part of Your breath,
my dreams are part of Your magnificent Projects.

Dear Jesus,
convert my aspirations into Your Designs,
my longings into part of Your Work,
so that I may make You known to the world
just as You, my Lord,
have let humankind know
the Greater Love of God.

May Your Kingdom, Lord, descend to Earth
so that each aspect of my consciousness
may be ennobled and transformed,
according to Your Word and Your infinite Mercy.

Keep me beside You, Jesus,
because in the dark night of the soul
I need to feel confidence and strength
in being able to be near You.

Allow me, Lord,
to empty myself completely by Your intervention
so that You may deposit in this small heart
the Work of Your Kingdom and Your whole Legacy
and thus the higher design of Your Spirit
may be fulfilled in this humanity.

Make me see with clarity and wisdom
the steps that today I must take towards You.

Sustain me with Your Hands
so that, with confidence, I may cross
the inner abysses that separate me from You.

Jesus,
make me recognize Your powerful Light,
make me recognize the sublime Fire of Your Heart,
so that You may be able to fulfill Your Divine Will in my life
forever.

Amen.

Third Poem

First Series - July 10, 2018

Empty me completely, Jesus,
even though my heart is not clean.

Comfort me during difficult moments
and reign everywhere with Your Power
so that it may be simpler for me to recognize You
in the brother and the sister who suffer,
in the sick soul,
in all those of whom You avail Yourself
so that within me may awaken the impulse of loving
in a way so similar to how You have loved.

Make me patient, Divine Jesus,
that in each circumstance of life
I may recognize the opportunity and the Grace
of transcending myself every day a little more.

Keep in my heart the ardor of Your purest desires
that the souls of the world may be able to know You
so that they may know the Kingdom of the Heavens.

Participate, Jesus, in each moment of life.
Make Yourself present, Lord,
both in our joy and in our deserts.
Make it so that I can be a witness of Your Word
and the fulfillment of Your redeeming Word.

That I may find in my path
the reason of living for You and in You
so that upon this planet
may be manifested the Sacred Project of God.

I confess today, Lord,
my weaknesses, failures and sorrows.

Transform it all, Lord,
according to Your Principle and Will
because the only thing I hope for
is to be happy for being by Your side
and to always reencounter You in the bliss of Communion,
in the joy of service and in the permanent and
unconditional giving of my heart.

After Your Gifts have purified me
inside and out, Lord,
send me wherever You most need me.
That in my life there may no longer be the freedom to choose
but rather the obedience of strictly following Your commands.

In this way, You will make me free of myself
because You, Lord, will be working
through this imperfect life
that hopes, beyond its dualities,
to consecrate itself to Your eternal and Sacred kind Heart.

Amen.

Fourth Poem

First Series - July 11, 2018

Above all, beloved Jesus,
liberate me from the chains and from the ties of desires
so that my human condition may be completely purified.

That by means of Your Body and Your Blood
I may reach the ennoblement of cells and of all matter.

May I become ever crystalline within Your Hands
so that You, my Lord,
may be able to use my consciousness
as a sacred mirror,
and all the attributes of Your Heart
may be poured into the souls of this humanity.

May the Love of Your Heart become known to the world
by means of the sacrifice of my life and of my whole consciousness.

For this, Lord, faithfully make me a partaker
of Your Sacred Sacraments
so that in each one of them
I may find a reason to make my life
each day more sacred and elevated.

Remove from my consciousness, dear Jesus,
these inferior aspects that dominate me and rule my life,
because I only hope and await that Your Divine Light
may become present in the deepest spaces and corners of my being
so that You may reveal to me the true reality of my consciousness
and in constant offering I may transform everything.

Make me similar to the apostles,
in consecration and in surrender.

Allow me, Lord, to demonstrate to You,
even in the small details,
how it is that I love You and how much I love You
through my brothers and sisters.

That all this not be a way or form
to boast my consciousness
and even less to make it shine before others.

Empty me of myself completely, Divine Jesus,
that in everything I may serve You.
But grant me the Grace of an anonymous and silent service
so that other hearts may find You before I do
and that I may only be a model
according to Your Principles and Designs.

Blessed Jesus,
convert all that which I do not manage to transform
and guide me until I am able to walk by Your side
with total trust and surrender.

Amen.

Fifth Poem

First Series - July 13, 2018

You expired, my Jesus, on the height of the Cross
and surrendered Your Spirit into the Hands of God.

Today, before Your merciful Presence,
I surrender to You my whole life, my soul and my will,
so that according to Your Principles of Love and Light
You may project into this small life
the sacred treasures of Paradise.

My Jesus,
make me always small and similar to You,
as You did with John, the apostle and prophet,
so that I may be able to know the greatnesses
of Your Mercy and of Your Pity.

Empty me completely from within
so that someday I may render myself to Your designs
with total openness and unconditional surrender.

Do not let me fall into temptation, Lord.

Liberate me from harassments,
liberate me from illusions.

Ignite within my soul
the sacred fire of the Holy Spirit.

Because thus I will make You known in the world,
just as You, my Spouse,
have made Yourself known
with all Your celestial mysteries
to my very tiny heart.

Help me, beloved Jesus,
to recognize Your Will
even in the smallest details.

Do not cease to guide me
and bless me in any moment.

Erase from my memory all mistakes
and fears of failure.

May I avail myself, Lord, of Your eternal confidence
so that one day I may be worthy
of witnessing Your Return.

Amen.

Sixth Poem

First Series - July 14, 2018

Lord,
may there be no time,
moment or preference
for me to want to look for You.

May I not exchange You, Lord, for anything or anyone.

I also ask You for this Grace,
because I know that You, beloved Lord,
know my weaknesses and uncertainties.

Fill me, Jesus,
with the most pure Source of Your truth and of Your transparency
so that some day I may learn to be so similar to You
in word, action and feeling.

Tear out from within me everything that may offend You
and, although it may hurt within,
do what You have to do, Lord,
and do not delay.

Take Your time
to project within me
Your most sacred designs.

Help me in the hours of great inner tempest.

Enlighten me in the moments of great tribulation.

Because I know, dear Jesus,
that in everything You are present
and that You will never abandon us,
in both the hardest moments of the desert
and the coldest tests of the inner winter.

Ignite in my chest, beloved Jesus,
the sacred flame of Your invincible Love
so that in the hour of the great inner battle
I may have absolute and full confidence
that You, Lord, will win.

Participate more and more
in this imperfect life.

Show me with clarity
and without self-illusions
what it is that I still have to change.

May I not drown within my own indifference.

On the contrary, Lord,
make me worthy of the atonement of Your Grace
so that I may transform everything
according to Your projects.

Amen.

Seventh Poem

First Series - July 15, 2018

Beloved Jesus,
may my confidence, although it may be poor, unite to Yours
so that Your Presence may strengthen my heart
in the tests that I will soon go through.

Beloved Son of God,
Servant of the Unchangeable Father,
make me small and simple in everything,
let me know the deepest mysteries
of Your Heart.

Reveal to me, Lord,
the intimacy of Your Soul
and the greatness of Your redeeming Love.

O Lord of the Universe!
that in the emptiness of my being
I may find the absolute surrender of my soul
so that some part of this imperfect being
may represent You on Earth
as a new apostle of Your Heart.

Beloved Jesus,
make me cherish and love my fellow beings,
just as You love me in an unconditional and eternal way.

Do not leave me stagnant in the shortcomings of the neighbor.

Rather, Lord, show me my shortcomings
so that according to Your Word and energy
I may be able to transform them.

I wish, Lord,
to see You reflected in the heart that suffers,
in the soul that despairs.

I wish to see You everywhere
and thus be able to participate in You
so that even the smallest gesture of my charity
may be able to quench the thirst that You feel
for the souls that do not accept You.

Give me bravery
and I will abandon myself into Your Arms.

Make me the instrument that You need.

Make me the project that You so much hope for
so that I may not interfere in anything, Lord,
but that it be You, Christ,
who works through this small life.

Amen.

Eighth Poem

First Series - July 16, 2018

Liberate me, Lord,
from the fear of any pain
that I may have to face.

May this liberation,
that only You will grant me through Your Grace,
help me to learn from suffering
and to not fear it.

Because I know, Lord,
that in everything there is a reason
and You, My Beloved, give us wisdom
to be able to understand it and accept it,
just as You silently and humbly accepted it
in the Garden of Gethsemane.

Grant me, Lord,
the opportunity of seeing
the holy redemption everywhere
and how the powerful Love of Your Heart
transforms all and cures all.

Stay with me, Lord,
in every moment,
at least until I learn
to recognize Your Will
and to fulfill it, step by step.

In the difficult and bitter moments
let me be close to You, just to contemplate You
in the luminous power of Your Holy Eucharist.

That by means of this offering, Lord,
I may find the strength and much courage,
every day, to overcome
my ideas, likes and satisfactions.

Make me surrender at Your Feet, Lord,
so that my pride,
vanity and arrogance may kiss them,
and all adversity or inner selfishness
may be dissolved by the balm of Your Light.

I trust in You, dear Jesus.
You, who know my weaknesses,
transform them all,
even though my sacrifice is just
a small grain of sand
in this vast Universe.

Amen.

Ninth Poem

First Series - July 17, 2018

Lord, although my soul
is poor and imperfect,
I beg You, beloved Jesus,
to avail Yourself of it
so that You may carry out
Your infinite and prodigious
Work of Love and Redemption.

Dear Jesus,
may this weak
and fragile soul be strengthened.

May Your Divine Fire, Lord,
lead me to some day find
the sacred Gift of Your innocence
so that,
according to the designs,
I too may be able to awaken
the Gift similar
to Your inner Purity.

Make me meek, Jesus.

Make me humble
and above all truthful
so that in these imperfect eyes
may be reflected Your loving and peaceful Gaze,
so that the most lonely and suffering souls
may find, through my offering,
Your powerful Celestial Presence.

For this, Lord,
liberate me from my desires,
liberate me from all ostentation and want.

That my heart be as simple as Yours.

Because my only wish, dear Jesus,
is to please You and share with You
the heavy Cross that You
still carry for the world.

Hear my supplication, Lord,
and make me once again
worthy of being before You.

Because, even though
I still do not understand
the power of Your mysteries,
I accept with love
all of Your Divine Wills.

May today Your Celestial Project
be fulfilled in me, Lord,
so that some day You can testify,
through me, Your Work of Redemption
before the Celestial Father.

Amen.

Tenth Poem

First Series - July 18, 2018

My Jesus, save me
from myself, from any action,
deed or thought
contrary to Yours.

Save me, Lord,
from my ideals
and from my own value judgements
so that I may represent You
according to Your Will.

Save me, Lord,
from all adversity,
interior and exterior.

Save me from all darkness
that may reign within me
and dissolve, with Your Power,
all that may be contrary
to Your Light and to Your Love.

Let me, Lord,
be able to recognize You
within my heart
as this love and this peace
that are unalterable,
perpetual and eternal,
rays that come from You
and that renew all things.

Allow me to render myself to You, Lord,
when I most need it,
and make me know the power
and the loving wisdom
of Your mysteries.

Keep me beside You
so that I may feel
the perfume of Your Love
and, above all,
the constant beat of Your Heart.

That in each sacrifice
my life may be renewed
and may be one more victory
for humanity and the planet.

That in each surrender
all may be offered in honor
to Your Divine and Eternal Heart.

Amen.

Eleventh Poem

First Series - July 19, 2018

Raise me from the ground, Lord,
even if I fall into temptation,
just as you raised Mary Magdalene
from the ground of perdition.

Liberate me, Lord,
from the harassments and attacks.

Temper my heart
so that I may receive from You
the strength that I now seek
and that I need.

Help me, my Beloved,
to find inner paradise.

Help me in the difficult and hard hours
to only look upon the horizon
so that for an instant
I may feel within me
Your Return.

May I feel, dear Jesus,
that every effort for You is worthwhile,
that despite the tempests,
internal and external,
You are always present,
imposing upon me
Your Sacred Hands
of blessing and healing.

And under the divine breath of the Holy Spirit,
dear Jesus,
may I have clarity and discernment
in the decisions of life.

May I never tire of seeking
the consecration to Your Divine Heart.

May in every moment
Your trust and Your Love invade me
so that I may learn like You,
beloved Lord,
to stand up from the ground
and continue, with patience,
carrying my own cross
until reaching the sacred victory
that Your redemption will give me.

Amen.

Twelfth Poem

First Series - July 21, 2018

It is in the most difficult hours
when I most need You, Lord,
so that you may liberate me from falling into temptation
and into the perverse sea of desires.

It is in the most difficult hours, beloved Lord,
when I most need You
so that You may teach me to come out,
in victory and humility,
from the inner tempest.

It is in the most difficult hours, Lord,
when I most seek You
so that You may reach out
Your sacred Hand towards me
and guide me along the path
that You are going through.

It is in the most difficult hours, Lord,
when I most call for You
so that Your Heart may be the beacon
that illuminates my paths,
and thus, I may avoid stumbling
upon my own shortcomings.

It is in the most difficult hours, Lord,
when I invoke You,
because I know that Your Spirit will save me
and come to assist Your sheep.

It is in the most difficult hours, Lord,
when I most implore You,
because, in spite of all the tests,
I know You will never abandon me
and that You will be by my side
to help me and comfort me.

In the most difficult hours, Lord,
I only seek the way and the means
of remaining in Your Sacred Heart,
because thus all adversity
and doubt will dissolve
and Your magnificent sovereignty
and Your majestic consoling Love will reign.

Amen.

Second Series of Poems

First Poem

Second Series - July 22, 2018

O Jesus!
sometimes it is difficult to remain
here, in this world,
amidst so many tests and temptations.

Sometimes, Lord,
I feel that I will not manage to reach You
because my own miseries
make me suddenly sink.

From all of this, save me, Lord,
I do not want to offend Your Heart
with all of that which sometimes
seems to have a life of its own within me.

Submerge me, Lord,
into the ocean of Your Mercy
because I know that thus You will purify me
of all my martyrdoms and condemnations
as many times as necessary.

Make disappear, dear Jesus,
this executioner that dwells within me,
that judges me, that frightens me
and that puts me in a place with no way out.

Help me, Jesus,
to be that which You so much hope for.

May I always be able to feel
thirst for You and for Your Presence
so that, someday, my entire being
may learn to become Your spouse.

Dear Jesus,
empty me of my human condition,
clean my inferior consciousness of so many shortcomings
and finally, Lord, place Your Peace
where I still do not manage to have it.

Because after all this inner struggle,
I know that You will triumph and make me worthy
of being able to be close to You forever,
serving You for all eternity.

Amen.

Second Poem

Second Series - July 23, 2018

I wish that, like You, beloved Lord,
I could understand the Divine Will
with absolute clarity,
as well as all the mysteries
that Your merciful Heart holds
about the infinite existence of this Universe
and of this Creation.

I wish, dear Jesus,
that I could surpass the limits of human consciousness
so that, within me, I might recognize
the inner universe and the spiritual riches
that God placed within each creature.

I wish, Lord,
that I were aware of this whole reality
beyond that which is concrete
so that even my cells
might awaken to the intelligence
and the knowledge that the Universe holds.

I wish, my Lord,
that I could receive this Grace
so that I might offer myself more consciously
as Your redeemed instrument
within the sublime Project of Your Mercy.

I ask You, Divine Jesus,
to empty me of myself
so that there may be a place, within me,
for the humility of Heaven,
which will make me simple and self-given
so that, perceptible to all of
Your Commands and Designs,
I may serve You.

Expand my consciousness
according to that which You have thought of.

I do not wish to flaunt
universal knowledge
but rather make it part of this consciousness
that implores You so that it may only
rise to the occasion.

I thank that You listen to me, Jesus,
and that You fulfill
Your Sacred Will within me.

Amen.

Third Poem

Second Series - July 24, 2018

I affirm it, Lord:
I know You can do everything in me,
although sometimes indifference or arrogance
may make me fall.

I know that You, Lord, can do everything,
and someday You will break
with Your own Hands
this hard stone of the human condition,
and on this day Your Glory, Lord,
will liberate me from all evil.

Meanwhile, Lord,
You, who know our
deepest miseries and errors,
I ask You, my Beloved,
make me a partaker of Your eternal Grace
so that I may be reborn
through the intercession of Your Sacred Heart.

Do not fail to show me the truth, Jesus.
However painful it may be, it will not be similar to
the pain of the nails that You endured
in Your most pure Hands.

Make me small
among the smallest,
make me invisible, Lord,
so that my arrogance
and my pride may disappear.

Hide me, Lord,
within Your luminous Wounds
and redeem
this whole imperfect being,
inside and out.

Because I know, my Jesus,
that someday You will triumph
and You will place me with all authority
where You most need me.

The hour has come, Lord,
for me to no longer be the one who lives
wishes, aspires or hopes,
but rather, dear Jesus,
the moment has come
for You to be in me.

Let me
die within, Lord,
just as Your humble Mother
died with You in each moment
at the foot of the Cross.

Reveal to me, Lord,
the incalculable value of Your Love
so that divested of everything
I may always say "yes" to You.

Amen.

Fourth Poem

Second Series - July 25, 2018

My Lord,
may the Rays of Your Heart
dissolve any possible
spiritual blindness within me
so that I may have the happiness
of recognizing Your humble steps.

Make me brave,
just as You were, dear Jesus,
in each step of the Cross.

May I not fear to carry
my own miseries,
may I fear not being able to find You.

But I know that as You are
kind and merciful, Lord,
You will grant me the Grace of finding You,
of feeling You and of recognizing You
in my inner world.

May You be this Divine Flame
within us
that transmutes and purifies everything.

Distance me, Lord,
from the illusions of life,
from everything that is superficial.

May I never lose the thirst
of drinking of Your Blood
and eating of Your Divine Body.

Make me similar to all
Your humble servants and martyrs
who gave until the last
minute of their lives
to recognize You and give testimony of You.

May I not fear the deserts
in which You may place me.

May I not fear the aridity
or the lack of sensitivity
or encouragement.

I only ask You, dearest Jesus,
that You renew me,
that You redeem me,
that You do in me
according to Your Word and Your Will,
because thus I will know the freedom
and the infinite joy
of serving You until the end.

Amen.

Fifth Poem

Second Series - July 26, 2018

Lord,
definitively liberate me
from my rotten miseries.

Wash me completely,
inside and out,
with the blessed Water
that springs from Your Sacred Heart.

Clean me and liberate me
from all atavisms
so that, renewed
by Your Spirit,
I may, once and for all, manage to
take the steps in Your redeeming Path.

Decompress the pressures of life.

My Jesus,
place Your holy Hands upon me
and, imposing the power
of all the Universe,
exorcise me, Lord,
so that finally I may
be liberated from the ties
and from all the prisons of life.

Keep me beside You, Lord.

Keep me close to You
and renew me constantly
and may I not lose the Grace
of transforming, day by day.

Under Your paternal Light,
close all uncertain doors
that may have been opened.

Close, within me,
any uncertain state
that separates me from Your Divine Love.

Grant me, Lord,
the opportunity of living You and of feeling You.

Grant me the Grace
of being able to be in communion with You
after having been purified.

Grant me the Mercy that I need
to be able to learn to forgive myself
and my brothers and sisters.

Build within me, Lord,
the New Brotherhood.

Amen.

Sixth Poem

Second Series - July 27, 2018

Lord,
hide me within Your Wounds
so that I may be purified of my mistakes.

Hide me, Lord,
within Your Wounds
so that I may receive the Divine Codes
of Transfiguration.

Lord,
hide me within your Wounds
so that spiritual Light
may invade me completely.

Lord,
hide me within Your Wounds
so that I may be protected from all evil
in order for Your powerful Peace to reign.

Lord,
hide me within Your Wounds
so that I may receive all Your Grace
and be deserving of Your unfathomable Mercy.

Lord,
hide me within Your Wounds
so that my soul may be a partaker
of the inner communion
with Your Divine Spirit
and all difficulties may dissipate.

Lord,
hide me within Your Wounds
so that I may know the profound essence
of Your Love and Your Compassion.

Lord,
hide me within Your Wounds
and make me a new instrument,
empty of everything and completely surrendered
to Your Sacred Heart.

Lord,
hide me within Your Wounds
so that Your sacred Humility
may awaken within me.

Amen.

Seventh Poem

Second Series - July 29, 2018

Prostrated before You, Lord,
I aspire to attain Your very simplicity so that
under this sovereign and loving spirit,
I may carry out Your Designs
and Wills.

Make me capable, Lord,
of loving all,
just as You, Sweet Shepherd,
love each one of Your sheep.

Give me, in trust,
the test that You
have thought of for me
so that I can grow in love
and dispel from my consciousness
all pride and arrogance.

Make me similar to Your servants,
available in love,
surrendered in service,
open to Your Mercy and Your Forgiveness.

May You be able
to deeply heal this being
and also reach the spaces
where I do not even manage to perceive reality.

I know that You, dear Jesus,
can do all.
Accept my offer, tiny
in comparison with the offer
of the entire Universe.

Convert within me
everything that is not well
and open the secure door for me
so that my soul may submerge
into the ocean of Your Divine Consciousness.

May I never stop smiling
at the life that God has given me.

Grant me, my Lord,
the strength of Your renewal
so that humanity may be renewed
in spirit and essence,
and thus we may live the so awaited
redemption.

Amen.

Eighth Poem

Second Series - July 30, 2018

O My Lord!
make me patient and persevering
just as You were
in each moment of Your Passion.

May I see, reflected in everything,
the Divine Will of God,
and even if sometimes it may seem unfair to me, Lord,
allow me to always
see the purpose of the Truth
that emanates in each deed.

Small and invisible, I want to be, Lord Jesus,
just as You made Yourself small
and simple in humanity.

May my steps reflect
the absolute trust
of being able to follow You.

Elevate my consciousness
in state and vibration
so that from now on,
beloved Jesus,
I may find the meaning
of everything that could happen.

May my inner hearing
not close; may it open,
just as my heart opens
to recognize Your Presence
in my brothers and sisters.

Help me, Lord,
to understand life
beyond what it seems to be.

Help me to experience
each test or obstacle
with the importance they have
for reaching the transcendence of my being.

Liberate me from myself,
in all senses and forms.

May You, my Jesus,
be the One who acts, proceeds
and manifests the Supreme Will
in order that, someday,
I may learn to die to myself
so that You, Sacred King,
may live in me
forever.

Amen.

Ninth Poem

Second Series - July 31, 2018

My Lord,
may I always be able to learn
from the culminating and difficult moments.

May I be able to learn
to see the luminous result
of each learning experience
so that I can grow internally
in humility, love and mercy.

Show me, Lord,
the greatness of each learning experience
and each test.

That in everything,
I may see the magnificence
that is Your Love and Your Mercy
so that we can learn
to humble and surrender ourselves to You
in each moment.

Participate, Lord,
in each school of life.

Enter into the depths
of this imperfect being
so that I myself
may discover the treasures of service
and of the good that You have placed
in my inner world.

Lord, unify me
constantly.

Make me small
but at the same time serving,
in all moments of life.

Deliver me to the world
as Your instrument
so that everyone may have the Grace
of knowing Your transforming
and vivifying Love.

Lord, do
what You have to do.

Amen.

Tenth Poem

Second Series - August 1, 2018

Liberate my soul, dear Jesus,
from all the inventions of the world,
may it awaken
to purity and compassionate love
by means of Your divine
and powerful intercession.

Lord, make me free
of resentments and guilt.

Build, through my service to You,
all the plans and gifts
that You, Beloved Lord,
have thought of.

Consecrate me to You, Lord,
even in the moments of test
and the challenges of life.

Make me a partaker
in the Sacrament of Reconciliation
and that every day I may
confess to You openly
so that my small spirit may be renewed
for as long as You,
Master of Love,
may consider.

Embrace me, Lord
during the cold nights.

Shelter me upon Your lap, Lord,
so that close to Your kind Heart
I may be able to adore You as the Great living and
divine Temple of God.

I give You thanks
for granting me Your eternal Peace.

Amen.

Eleventh Poem

Second Series - August 2, 2018

Jesus, Savior and Redeemer,
make me humble and similar
to the angels of Heaven.

Make me similar to them
in obedience and in service
so that my whole imperfect consciousness
may have the Grace of, someday, being part
of the Law of the Hierarchy.

Help me and teach me,
through examples,
to respect and revere my brothers and sisters
so that there may be built in our consciousnesses
the sacred spirit of brotherhood
and unity.

Allow me, Lord,
to fervently embrace
each cross that I am to carry
so that humanity and the world
may be relieved of its errors.

May we all, Lord Jesus,
have the happiness of participating
in Your Presence in the Eucharist,
in Communion as well as in Confession.

May we all, as brothers and sisters,
feel and encounter the Great Priest of Love
so that we may commune
of His precious Divine Energy.

For this, Lord,
wash my face with the Water of Your Fount.

Purify my hands, my head and my feet
with the sacred Water
that once sprang from Your Side
and may I, just like the Roman soldier
who wounded Your Heart,
be bathed by the powerful Light
of Your Christic Cells.

Convert me into the apostle that You need
and make me small in everything
so that I may always
recognize
Your Truth.

Amen.

Twelfth Poem

Second Series - August 3, 2018

My Lord and Celestial King,
reveal to me, in this life,
the projects that You have thought of
for my consciousness.

That, in truth and in sincerity,
I may be able to respond
to Your Designs every day
in order to manifest on Earth
the Divine Will.

Dear Jesus,
make me free of everything
that compromises my consciousness
so that I can take steps towards You.

Empty me constantly
so that I may have the Grace
of receiving Your most immaculate
and pure Celestial Principles.

And even if my consciousness
does not come close to the truth,
due to incapacity or some other reason,
I ask You, Lord, to help me
find the perfect meaning
of Your Designs so that,
as an apostle and servant of Yours,
I may represent on Earth
the testimony of redemption.

Remove from my heart
all feelings of vainglory.

Make me small and simple,
just as Your Spirit, Lord,
is simple and small.

Because if I am full
of Your consoling Love, Lord,
I will be able to share it and,
by means of the example
of service and charity, transmit
the vivifying force
that You provide us with,
time after time.

I offer You this moment, Lord,
so that it may be contemplated
as the true offering
of my human heart.

Amen.

Third Series of Poems

First Poem

Third Series - August 7, 2018

Jesus,
what shall I do with so many
Graces within my consciousness?

I ask You, beloved Lord,
make me worthy of receiving them,
one by one.

Make my heart small and humble
so that I may have the happiness
of knowing Your Wonders.

You know, dear Jesus,
that I am not worthy
of so many mercies.

Help me to deepen into love,
as You did
in each step of Calvary.

How is it possible to love
that which would be unforgivable, Lord?

Tear out from my being
all pride and arrogance.

That in each moment,
dear Master,
I may be able to sustain myself in You
so that I may have enough bravery
to surpass
my own feelings,
my hardest resistances
and all the obstacles
that separate me from You
and from Your Truth.

May I be able to humble myself
as many times as needed
so that in the resignation
of my personality,
beloved Lord,
I can transform
the human condition
that has always condemned
and punished me.

Sacred Liberator of life,
Blessed Jesus!
make me nothing in every moment
and submit me to Your unchanging Will
so that any trace
of personal power may vanish
from my consciousness and thus I may be able to live
Your magnificent Will.

Amen.

Second Poem

Third Series - August 8, 2018

Lord of Kindness,
placate the injustice
that is shown
before Your Eyes.

Relieve the inner pain
of those who truly suffer.

Place Your consoling Love
into the sick souls
and do not cease to guide me,
not even for a moment.

Beloved Jesus,
You know we are weak
and fragile of spirit,
You know we wound Your Heart
time and again with our
indifferent acts,
You know we do not do what we could
but rather we do what we should not.

Patient and beloved Jesus,
enter deeply
into our hearts
and tear out from us
all pride and arrogance
so that, free from the prisons of life,
we may humbly learn
to console You and adore You.

Sustain us during our falls.

Protect us in our weaknesses,
and always liberate us from ourselves
so that we may be worthy
of honoring and glorifying You
as the Savior and Redeemer
of our lives.

May we not abandon You.

May we abandon ourselves in You, Lord,
so that Your Sacred Will may be fulfilled.

Amen.

Third Poem

Third Series - August 9, 2018

Lord,
that in spite of my faults,
my heart and may soul may achieve
the Grace of being able to serve You
with plenitude, bliss and love.

Help Me, Lord,
to overcome the atavisms of life.

May Your divine and powerful Light
shine within all spaces.

May my steps
be blessed by You, Lord.

Open the door for me
so that I may submerge
into Your Sacred Heart
and thus, I may forget myself
and the world.

Take me away, Lord,
from temptations,
from imminent deceits
and from all dangers.

May I learn to Christify myself
by means of the same patience
and the same silence that You,
dear Jesus,
expressed during
the first moments
of Your difficult agony.

May I manage to recognize You
in the heart of each brother and sister
so that human appearances
may disappear.

Teach me to be humble
in service,
faithful in prayer,
truthful in word
and resigned before
any test and humiliation.

Lord, deposit into my heart
Your innermost treasures
and forever transform
this imperfect life
so that it may serve
as Your model
and as an instrument for
Your redeeming Work.

Amen.

Fourth Poem

Third Series - August 10, 2018

Lord,
may my soul be capable
of achieving transparency
in consecration.

May I not tire
of taking steps towards You, my Lord,
so that I may gradually abandon
all that which time and again
separates me from You.

Make me
divested of self, Lord.

May Your feeling of Love
and Mercy for the neighbor
be my feeling of love
and mercy for others.

Liberate me from the heavy chains
that make me regress
and do not allow me to move forward.

Liberate my heart, Lord,
from all evil, betrayal and disdain.

May I learn to sustain myself in You
so that I may manage to represent You
on the surface of the Earth.

Dear Jesus,
make me see everything beyond,
as it truly is.

Make me understand my fellow being,
just as You understood and accepted
those who rejected You, martyrized You and humiliated You
at the foot of the Cross.

Help me, Lord,
to live unconditional
and Christic Love.

Help me to surpass
the layers of appearances
and may I be able to see You
in each human heart.

Amen.

Fifth Poem

Third Series - August 11, 2018

Lord,
bathe me inside and out
with the fount of Your Grace.

Purify each aspect of my being
so that I may always be able to renew myself
through You.

Purify me of my thoughts
and of my feelings.

I ask You, our Lord,
to be part of my being.

Teach me to be patient
and persevering in every moment.

Teach me to be humble
and simple before others
so that my personality
may not seek to promote itself in anything
but rather be willing to serve
when I am needed and called.

Lord of Truth,
may my feelings be ennobled,
may my word rise in vibration
and may each prayer that I offer You
be able to be received in Heaven
as a drop of light in the vast Universe
so that the Graces of God
may continue to descend.

Teach me to offer my life to service.

Teach me to offer my heart
as an instrument of healing.

Teach me, dear Jesus,
to empty me of myself day by day
so that each step that I take
may be blessed by Your consoling Love.

May my life be guided
and protected by You, Lord,
and may the Holy Spirit descend
so that I may fulfill,
within Your majestic Work,
all the Designs that You have thought of
within Your humble Heart.

Amen.

Sixth Poem

Third Series - August 12, 2018

May I become
like a child, Lord,
so that I may
always be upon Your lap.

May I become
like a child, Lord,
so that I may grow
in simplicity and in humility.

That, as a child in spirit,
I may recognize
how wonderful and sublime
it is to remain in You, Lord.

That, like a child, I may recover
the attributes of Your Heart
so that I may represent You
as Your child and as Your companion.

That now, being able to be
in Your humble Arms, Lord,
I may closely come to know
the sacred mysteries
of Your Heart and of Your Word.

May I be invaded,
beloved Lord,
by Your Divine Spirit
so that I may sincerely fulfill
the attributes of Your Consciousness.

Renew me always, Lord.

I know You accept our offering.

Receive me into Your Kingdom
of Love and Redemption
so that with the Father
we may celebrate Your celestial Glory.

Amen.

Seventh Poem

Third Series - August 14, 2018

Elevate my soul to Heaven, Lord,
so that it may unite to Yours
and thus commune of Your Divinity.

Make me simple and true
in daily tasks.

Deposit into my heart
the power of Your Trust
and make this life an instrument
in the Hands of God.

Allow me, Lord,
to live in the void and to witness
in each act of love
Your celestial Paradise.

Avail Yourself of my consciousness
so that the Universe
may descend to Earth
and everything, absolutely everything,
may be transformed.

Let me know
the deep meaning of Your Word, Lord.

Elevate my consciousness
as many times as necessary
so that I may be awake
before Your call.

Help me to vanquish arrogance
and spiritual pride so that,
free from any blindness,
I may receive Your blessing
to have awareness and discernment.

Keep me by Your side
and I will be able to keep in my inner world
the magnificence of what it means to be in You, Lord.

Make my life that which You so hope for.

The time has come for me to cross
the portal towards redemption,
thus I will be able to accompany You
as a servant of Yours
and as a disciple of Your Heart.

Amen.

Eighth Poem

Third Series - August 16, 2018

Relieve me from my sorrows, Lord.

Please, Master,
may Your divine Love be reborn within me.

Make me humble and simple each day
so that I may not lose the fortitude
of always sustaining myself in You.

Allow me, Lord,
to love more deeply.

May the divine Love that You teach us
help me to abandon indifference.

May my heart and my life, dear Jesus,
be true representations
of the Work of Your Redemption.

In adoration,
may I feel You and reencounter You.

Within each step that
I must take towards You, Lord,
may I have enough courage to do so,
and may I live enough humility
in order to carry it out.

My Lord, Celestial King,
visit the temple of my soul,
consecrate it to Your Divine Spirit
so that my whole being may be an instrument
of Your magnificent Work.

Leave my feet bare of the past,
of rancor and resentments.

Wash me, Lord,
with the nonmaterial Water
of Your Fount and thus I will be renewed
because You will have granted me
Your Grace and Your Mercy.

Amen.

Ninth Poem

Third Series - August 17, 2018

Lord Jesus Christ,
when anguish comes,
may I not fear my own purification
or that of my fellow beings.

May the glorious flame of Your Love
fill us completely
so that we have the inner strength
to overcome ourselves.

Lord Jesus, teach us to live
in the same way that You lived
the Eternal Father in each moment.

That we be able to be ambassadors of Your Legacy.

That we be able to represent You on Earth
just as You deserve it, so that
we may cease to disappoint Your Heart
and we may fill It with bliss and joy
through fulfilling
Your Designs, step by step.

Make our hearts brave,
willing to suffer for You,
and thus that we be able to repopulate the Earth
with new values of brotherhood
and mercy.

May each test that You send us, Lord,
help us to confirm our fortitude within You.

We ask You, dear Jesus,
to make us like You in humility,
true in charity and peaceful
in the face of the attacks of life.

May we not fear to humble ourselves before You, Lord,
as many times as You need it,
because some day we hope to be nothing
and in this nothing merge ourselves into God forever.

Amen.

Tenth Poem

Third Series - August 18, 2018

Beloved Jesus,
make me brave in each moment.

May the tests serve
to purify my consciousness.

May the challenges that You send me
help in the transcendence of my being.

May each transition of life
be the passage towards a new
state of consciousness.

Help me, Lord,
to be persevering,
humble and dedicated.

May I be able to feel within my heart
the Ray of Your Mercy
and the divine and supreme Grace
acting and working throughout my being
because thus Your divine Light will triumph
before the inner darkness
of these times.

Lord Jesus,
strengthen me day after day
in the union with You,
make me small and similar to You
so that I may perfectly imitate You
in each step.

Empty me in every moment, Lord.

Rejoice my soul
while being in Your glorious Presence.

And I ask You, Lord,
to relieve the weight of my cross
so that, with Your merciful assistance,
I may surrender completely
at the Feet of the Celestial Father.

Amen.

Eleventh Poem

Third Series - August 19, 2018

Lord, grant me
the Grace of humility
through Saint Joseph.

May my feet find this path
so that, more each day,
I may be able to serve You in joy and in surrender.

That together with Saint Joseph
I may carry out the Designs of God
so that the planet may be repopulated
with love and hope.

Lord, make me so humble
and small in all of Your Works.

Take us, my brothers and sisters and I,
along the paths of love
so that we may be blessed and touched
by Your Divine Mercy.

Amen.

Twelfth Poem

Third Series - August 20, 2018

O beloved Jesus!

How long has it been that I walk
along this pathway of the planet
in search of Your humble Footprints
in order to be able to imitate Your Path!

O my Lord, Master of Love!

How long have I been
in search of Your Heart
to be able to feel It, live It and adore It
with the honor that You deserve!

O Lord Jesus,
sweet Spouse of Truth!

Magnificent Man of Nazareth!

How I have looked for Your Spirit
in daily Communion!

How I have aspired
to carry out Your Will
to be able to concretize it!

Dear Master of Light,
finish dissipating from within me all illusions
and may I be able to share with all
the wonderful Love
of which You have so much given me.

I wish that many more hearts
would be encouraged to pass through Your healing Fire.

I wish that Heaven and Earth
knew how much I love You
and how much I need You.

Make the mystery of Your Resurrection known to me.

May each moment experienced by You in the Passion
remain kept in my essence
until I am able to renew my life within You.

Amen.

Association Mary
Mother of the Divine Conception

Founded in December of 2012, at the request of the Virgin Mary, Association Mary, Mother of the Divine Conception, is a religious association without ties to any institutionalized religion. It has a philosophical-spiritual, ecumenical, humanitarian, charitable, cultural character, and it supports all activities that are indicated through the instructions transmitted by Christ Jesus, the Virgin Mary, and Saint Joseph.

Association Mary encourages a true ecumenical cooperation and a fraternal relationship among religions by means of prayer and altruistic service.

Contributions, in all their manifestations: monetary, material resources and volunteer work, make it possible for its activities to be free of charge, maintained and expanded.

For more information, visit:
www.divinemessengers.org

Grace Mercy Order

An autonomous Christian and ecumenical religious organization, without formal ties to any institutionalized religion. It proposes monastic living through consecrated life, based on the teaching of Christ.

Founded in 2009, the Order seeks to unconditionally offer itself as an instrument of Divine Work, in communion with human beings and all other Kingdoms of Nature. It is a proposal for fraternal and community life, consecrated to peace, prayer, the good and selfless service.

Irdin Publishing Association

An institution at the service of the expansion of consciousness.
Its goal is to propagate works of a philosophical-spiritual
nature in these times of global transformations and of great
need for inner search. With teachings that present keys
for the acknowledgment of the nonmaterial laws that govern
the universe in which we live and sustain the Earth,
it invites us to unravel the mysteries of our planet's history
and enter into paths of peace.

Irdin is a non-profit publishing house
run by volunteer collaborators.

For more information, visit:
www.irdin.org.br

Shasti Association

Shasti Association is a non-profit organization, located in Mount Shasta, California, United States, dedicated to the dissemination of philosophical-spiritual teachings that include those of traditional wisdom and evolutionary meaning. Shasti Association is responsible for the English publications of the entire Work of José Trigueirinho Netto and his collaborators. Thus, Shasti Association offers an important impulse for the diffusion of this work throughout the North American continent and countries where the use of the English language is predominant. It also collaborates with Irdin Publishing in the dissemination of the Work of Paul Brunton in Portuguese.

Visit the website:
www.shasti.org